GENERATING WEALTH

Thinking is the leader and mother of achievement. Ideas are the mother of inventions.

By

Ernest Sarfo

Generating Wealth

Author: Ernest Sarfo

Copyright © 2025 Ernest Sarfo

The right of Ernest Sarfo to be identified as author of this work has been asserted by the author in accordance with section 77 and 78 of the Copyright, Designs and Patents Act 1988.

ISBN 978-1-83538-735-1 (Paperback)
      978-1-83538-736-8 (E-Book)

Cover Design and Book Layout by:
    White Magic Studios
    www.whitemagicstudios.co.uk

Published by:
    Maple Publishers
    Fairbourne Drive, Atterbury,
    Milton Keynes,
    MK10 9RG, UK
    www.maplepublishers.com

All rights reserved. No part of this book may be reproduced or translated by any form or by any means, electronic or mechanical, including photocopying, recording or by any information storage and retrieval system without written permission from the author

The book is a work of fiction. Unless otherwise indicated, all the names, characters, places and incidents are either the product of the author's imagination or used in a fictitious manner. Any resemblance to actual people living or dead, events or locales is entirely coincidental, and the Publisher hereby disclaims any responsibility for them.

DEDICATION:

This book is dedicated to the Grace of God that impacted me with a deep sense of revelation knowledge through an inspired relationship that span many years of mentorship and guidance.

It's been a studious warming relationship which will forever be memorable.

CONTENTS

Dedication: 3

Introduction 5

Generating Ideas And Vision 7

Goal Setting 56

Finding A Market: Asking Through Advertising 64

Managing Successful Ideas Of Wealth 71

When Ideas Of Wealth Are Blessed: 81

Keep Good Conduct: Integrity 86

Develop A Giving Habit: 91

Other Books From The Author 96

Author's Bio: 97

Acknowledgements 98

INTRODUCTION

Given the opportunity, everybody wants to be wealthy. It's a good thought. But we've got to have the right perspective to achieve it. No one cruises to success. You have to work towards it with creativity, diligence and hard work.

Wealth can be defined as "an abundance of valuable possessions or money" or "plentiful supplies of a particular resource or desirable thing".

Wealth and income are not the same, though they are related. Whilst wealth deals with the level of abundance of assets you have or plentiful supply of them, income is the amount that comes into your hands in a certain period of time, for example, like salary or wages. However, plentiful savings of income becomes wealth deposit, which can be a potential source of investments to generate continuity of wealth.

Wealth and comfort: Though it does not determine life, being wealthy is needed in life because it gives you leverage or the ease to meet your needs and wants. It brings comfort, and makes you happy when it comes to the realm of reaching out to your material needs and wants.

I have not met anyone who says that being poor is good. It cannot be good because it denies you the ability to enjoy the juicy part of life, not to mention that your health and longevity in life can be short-circuited.

But know that no individual person jumps to success, you have to find a way to generate wealth to enjoy its worth.

The aim of this book is to impact your life, and throw some light on generating wealth from a Godly perspective.

GENERATING IDEAS AND VISION

Generating wealth is about the ability to use your imagination to develop ideas, and create a vision of products or services, that people will need, and want to buy.

Human existence, and the world we live in, including the air we breathe, the rainfall and the animals and birds are the results of someone's ideas. They did not just magically appear.

The power of imagination is a divine, intrinsic, creative ability in us.

Desires, talents, gifts are naturally embedded in our creative nature. These create passions in us to imagine, what you want to do and who you want to become. These qualities arouse purpose in life, for us to pursue a dream, until accomplished.

Purpose is the reason why something exists. For example, the manufacturer of a product is the first person, who knows the reason for producing it. He is the first person to conceive the thought and execute it.

Awareness of this can make you set aside, an alone time to think and imagine what you want to be, and what you want to do, what ideas you can create to put a product or a service on the market.

How we were created: The world we live in, as well as the human beings who live in it, are the ultimate results of someone's ideas.

According to scriptural references, the idea was to create an environment or an atmosphere that human beings can live in comfort. So, God created the earth by imagining an idea of, first, a sky with planets including the Sun, and the Moon, with a weather system that will form a canopy of support for human activities on the earth, where air to breathe, rainfall, and sunshine will interplay to make life possible. The second thought was to create human families in His image, with a creative mind, i.e. to be like Him and live happily on earth with joy and fun. That gave Him humans in life to have fellowship with and to manage, after seeing to it that everything He had made was very good and beautiful (Genesis 1:1-31). That was God's initial idea in a vision that was imagined. That gave Him a world with success, as we see today in our lives.

HOW TO DEVELOP IDEAS:

- **We are created to think and imagine ideas.** Successful people develop the habit of setting aside solitary moments to think, alone time for themselves and meditate on ideas, behind closed doors, and use their imagination to design their future. Your ideas decide your actions and progress. Thinking over ideas, and meditating upon them are the fundamentals of successful people and it begins with an awareness of yourself to do just that.

Your sense of imagination is a natural powerful tool, that must be used because it not only gives an immediate overview of your future, but also envisions possibilities that can be turned into reality.

We are naturally endowed with talents, and gifts, and with an intelligent quotient (IQ) which impact our desires and passions to generate ideas through imagination and visualize designs. All these happen when you pause to take moments, to think in private, and imagine what idea to create to put something in the public domain that will impact the lives of others in the market. When such people are impacted, it creates a reciprocal action from the people to the "idea thinker," because they will buy more of what you create, to make the life of the producer better in wealth creation. So, it is a two way process or movement, you reap what you sow.

Your ideas and what you produce can be your niche in the market world: A niche is your specific, specialized zone of an idea well-suited to you, or your talent, especially to break through in the market. What you are able to achieve in private, is what you come out with in public. Wealth does not come at random. You generate it.

- **WORTHY OF NOTE: Thinking is the leader and mother of achievement. Ideas are the children of thinking and the producers of products and services in all establishments and industries.**

- **As children grow up to become mothers, so have ideas become the mother of invention.**

We must find time to stop running, stop behaving like "busy bees," and find time to think about ideas to create. You are what you desire and think of. As a man thinks in his heart, so is he. Give yourself permission to dream ideas. They are the 'Seeds of creativity' and also brand names.

There is nothing wrong in thinking outside the realm of possibility. It stretches your faith and imagination especially if you are a believer of faith in God. Wealth is big, and God being Super-Big, will always expect us to imagine big, because we are created in His image.

We are told to ask big, "Ask of Me, and I will give you the nations for your inheritance, and the ends of the earth for your possession."(Psalm 2:8)

Such a statement is a sign of something big and beyond the realm of human strength and possibility. It implies, ask me things that make me feel like God. It is about us aligning our faith with the Supernatural. It is at this point that we receive divine aid or support.

- **There is also the concept of acquiring your ideas, and deciding to use them to work in someone's else successful, functioning ideas to also create wealth:** not all are able to invest in capital generating investments, but can decide to use their ideas to join someone with similar ideas who is successful in that business. Through that, it helps that person to also build a wealthy future along the way. These are what I call life's stepping stones.

- **There is also the idea of capital Investment opportunities:** This comes when you have some savings. It would happen that some corporate body of investors that may be doing well can attract you with an idea of investment opportunities. You can become shareholders in such places. You can create a portfolio for shares, and buy different types of shares, from a range of different companies and keep getting profits as dividends, or an opportunity to sell some for profit when the price is right.

All these come under the concept called diversification of capital.

- **You must have the passion to create your desires with the hope of generating wealth.** What you behold, you become, as your mind and heart transform it into passion. What you consistently attach importance to, becomes a part of you, it possesses you.

- **You may also enrol in a course to study or self-study at home** to acquire knowledge of what you think of doing to widen your scope of imagination or your desires.

- **Take time to associate with or study those who are successful** in the areas of your desires and choices: they become your mentors.

- **Talents and Gifts are doors of ideas and creativity:** a man's gift makes room for him, and brings him before great men. They make you creative to excel in those areas. Find time to think about the talents and gifts you possess, and invest in yourself. Success begins with thinking and imagining things that can be developed.

- **Direct God spoken, inspired ideas are golden keys to success:** sometimes

God gives you direct, spoken ideas to create something for the market. It can be a service or management ideas as He gave to one person named Joseph in ancient Egypt, for him to become the Governor in those days. At other times, it may be ideas to make products, as He did for Jacob of ancient history in which, as a sheep breeder, he was able to cause the sheep to produce spotted and streak coloured type in greater dimensions. Those sheep were his wages according to an agreement, which he made with his uncle Laban, who happened to be the owner of the livestock farm business.

- **A typical close example of idea creation:** The story is told by one motivational speaker Terri Savelle Foy, that there was a lady who wanted to raise $100,000 to start her own advertising agency, because she was dissatisfied with the job she was doing.

She found a niche or a gap in the market to develop an idea that will meet her need. Initially she began asking people around her, as to how she could raise $100,000 in 90 days. Fortunately, she got the advice to write a book that will appeal to the needs of people and sell in 90 days. She imagined that if she could sell 100,000 copies even for a dollar each, the target would be achieved. She asked around to find out, that the bestselling books in America were about "weight loss," especially among the women. Next, in order to distinguish hers from the other books, she began to ask among the women at the market places, as to which part of their body they urgently wanted to lose weight. She got the unanimous response, "my thigh". So, she wrote a book called "Thinning Thighs in 30 days," with the photo of a female's thin thighs on the front cover of the book." She released the book in April and by end of June, she had accrued $100,000. She asked her way out to success. The idea of asking is a principle for success.

WORTHY OF NOTE: Business is about your ability to identify and satisfy what others will need or look for. That will be your niche or gap in the market.

WHAT YOU IMAGINE TO DO BECOMES YOUR VISION: Imagination gives you ideas to create a Vision of what to do and who you want to be known as.

You need to have a vision in life otherwise, when you are ignorant or refuse to act, you may end up going around in circles, and can suffer stagnation.

EXAMPLE: In ancient Israel, a people who were destined for a promised land of comfort and prosperity, ended up circling around in the wilderness for a journey that should have taken them eleven days : "For the children of Israel walked forty years in the wilderness, till all the people who were men of war, who came out of Egypt, were consumed, because they did not obey the voice of the Lord—to whom the Lord swore that He would not show them the land, which the Lord had sworn to their fathers that He would give them, "a land flowing with milk and honey."

Their vision became a circling around, instead of aiming at reaching the promised land with a mind-set of determination.

VISION CAPTIVATES SUCCESS:

What you have faith for; you conceive it in your mind. When conception becomes an obsession, you will manifest it into reality in life. What you think about, you end up bringing it about.

In ancient Israel, whilst in captivity Nehemiah heard of the destruction of his city Jerusalem and the distress of his people, it birthed forth a dream of desire and purpose, and it created an assignment for him to seek the then foreign King's favour for resources of wealth and the mandate to go and rebuild the city. With passion burning in his heart, he made a request and favour was granted him successfully. **He nursed a Vision of trust in God,** and with faith it paid off tremendously.

As a man thinks in his heart, so does he becomes. What you think about, you bring about. **You become what you constantly keep before you, and review consistently.** (Proverbs 23:7)

A person without a specific vision doesn't get a settled and purposeful life. A person's vision is always related to their heart's desire and purpose in life.

DECISION MAKING AND PLANNING STRATEGIES: imagination stems from decision and planning. You decide to think and imagine ideas.

- Your approaches must be ideas of what to create: think and imagine of what you can do and put on the market. Your talents and gifts will always stir up a passion in you.

- Decide on where to focus first, don't jam things together. De-clutter the crowded flashy thoughts. Do not have too many things to do together. Planning and dedication get things done.

- Have the attitude of success, be positive minded.

- Invest in yourself: What do you spend time on and who do you spend time with? Read, study about your gifts and talents. Find out knowledge about what you want to do. Gather intelligence about it. For lack of knowledge and understanding, potential dreams die.

- Think efficiently and take precautions for longevity.

- What you envision to do, becomes your dream in life, that's your vision.

- In other words, find your niche in the market. Your niche is defined as "a specialized segment of the market that needs your particular kind of product or service."

SOME SUCCESSFUL INDIVIDUALS: Some business Owners and CEO's who have achieved success in generating business ideas include:

- **Bill Gates and Paul Allen,** coming up with the idea of "Microsoft." The name Microsoft comes from the words "microcomputer" and "software". Microsoft became one of the biggest tech companies in the world, and is still a leader in software development.

- **Elon Musk,** Known as the co-founder of PayPal, founder of Space X, a significant investor in Tesla, and the person who acquired Twitter (now X) in 2022.

- **Jeff Bezos,** (Amazon), The Amazon Company is now a worldwide company that deals with a range of parcel delivery solutions, including Amazon Shipping, Amazon Flex and Amazon Logistics. These services cover both small and large business enterprises, including those placed on other online platforms.

- **Mark Zuckerberg,** (Facebook), this is now a popular social media Company

- **Dyson's British strawberries Farming,** with its latest modern technology, produces 750 tonnes of strawberries each year for British consumers, in a way that is able to feed the population and limit strawberry imports.

- **Oprah Winfrey,** (Oprah's media empire). Oprah hit the limelight in America with her 'Oprah Winfrey Talk Show'. With the popularity of the Talk Show as well as interviewing celebrities, everything she touched became gold, resulting in a net worth of over $2.5 billion. She later created a media empire where she formed her Company Harpo Production, producing films like 'Colour purple' and 'Beloved'. She also launched 'The Oprah Magazine', as well as 'Oprah Winfrey Cable TV Network, which showed peoples lifestyle etc. She is a significant share in such Companies like Weight Watchers, thus making the Company more popular to boost its market share in the weight lost industry.

- **Steve Jobs** (Apple), played a vital role in Apple's Company development of personal computers, mobile phone devices and much more. He championed the development of popular products like the Macintosh, iPod, iPhone, and iPad, thus bringing unchallenged innovations into the industries. He was a visionary leader who became a driving force for Apple to become a global name and a 'technology guru'. He was an authority in the field of technology.

- **Richard Branson (Virgin Group):** Richard Branson is an achiever, a highly successful business investor, who stands at the behest of the Virgin Group. It has 40 Companies now operating in 35 countries in various industries. Richard's zeal for entrepreneurship began with the magazine 'Student', then he later transitioned to Virgin Mail Order Records and to Virgin Records. His love for Investment has since enabled him to branch out into new industries like airlines (Virgin Atlantic), telecommunications (Virgin Mobile), Virgin Railways in London and later space travel (Virgin Galactic). His success story is an exciting movement to inspire others.

- **The Aircraft flying idea: The Wright Brothers' Journey to Fly an Engine-Powered Aircraft.**

We know of the two brothers who first started to develop engine-powered flying aeroplanes, the Wright brothers from Ohio, USA. Growing up, the brothers were curious about flying. They were fascinated by the mechanics of their favourite playing toy, which was modelled like a helicopter and powered by a rubber band that spun its blades intermittently. The brothers started a business together and decided one day to build a flying aircraft powered by an engine. That was a journey of adventure and risk, and their determination never waned until they achieved their goal. After several tests with kites and gliders, in 1903, they were able to manufacture a gasoline-engine-powered aircraft whose propellers were wooden. After several unsuccessful attempts, they fortified the parts with extra fabrics, and finally, in 1903, they succeeded in flying the world's first piloted engine aircraft. They are today the inspirers of modern aviation, which has paved the way for modern adventures and latest technologies in aeroplane developments. It all started with an idea and a bond in a relationship to make it to the top, and they succeeded because they kept the idea as a journey to complete.

- **Jacob and Special Divine Ideas**

In ancient Israel, God sold a business idea to one called Jacob. This young man had a vision in dreams where he saw, that the rams which were mating with the flock were "spotted, speckled and striped," essentially giving Jacob the idea to strategically breed his livestock to produce more spotted and speckled animals, which he then used to outsmart his cheating father-in-law Laban, by ensuring only the spotted animals were born to his flock, because that was the ultimate agreement.

Based on this vision, Jacob was given an idea to take fresh-cut branches from poplar, almond and chestnut trees and make white stripes on them by peeling the bark, and exposing the white inner wood of the branches.

Then he placed the peeled branches in all the watering troughs, so that they would be directly in front of the flocks when they came to drink. When the flocks were in heat and came to drink, they mated in front of the branches. And they bore young ones that were streaked or speckled or spotted. Thus the man became exceedingly prosperous, and had large flocks, female and male servants, and camels and donkeys.

This story is often interpreted as a demonstration of God's providence, allowing Jacob to prosper even while being treated unfairly by his uncle Laban, who changed the concept of the agreement several times because he did not want Jacob to gain any advantage over his wealth.

- **The Joseph divine idea that shot him from prison into splendour:** In ancient Egypt, there was this young man, Joseph, who was sold into slavery by his brothers, because he kept having dreams of greatness in which he kept seeing his brothers and all the family bowing to him. That infuriated the brothers and they found an opportunity in the field while the sheep were grazing to sell Joseph as a slave to some Merchants going to Egypt.

Some 13 years later, famine hit that part of the world for seven years, and the only place they heard that food was available in plentiful supply, was in Egypt. So they made the journey to buy food to stock. Fortunately, but, unfortunately for them, when they got there their brother Joseph was the Governor in Egypt, and the one directly in charge of selling and distributing the food store of grains. You can imagine the embarrassment and fear created by the scene.

How come that this slave boy is the Governor or in this modern era, the Prime Minister of the Country Egypt? Let me tell you what happened.

When the boy was taken to Egypt, the Merchants sold him to a captain of Egypt called Portiphar. Joseph prospered greatly in the house as everything he touched, became a blessing to the captain. Not long after, the wife of Portiphar began to cast desirous eyes on Joseph as she found him a handsome young man. However, when he refused to sleep with her, she falsely accused Joseph of attempting to rape her, and reported the matter to the husband. That infuriated the husband and got Joseph into prison. Sometime after, the then King, called Pharaoh, had a disturbing and terrifying dream. He later found out, that the only person who could interpret the dream was the one in prison. So Joseph was called for, and this is how the dream was interpreted:

These were the words of Joseph - - - "God has shown you, King Pharaoh, what he is going to do. There will be seven years of great plenty in all the land of Egypt. After that, there will be seven years of famine, and all the good years will be forgotten, because the famine will ruin the country. The time of plenty will be entirely forgotten, because the famine which follows will be so terrible.

The repetition of your dreams means God is seeking your attention to alert you, that the situation is certain and that it will surely happen in the near future.

Now you should choose some man with wisdom and insight, and put him in charge of the country. You must also appoint other officials and take a fifth of the crops during the seven years of plenty. Order them to collect all the food during the good years that are coming, and give them the authority to store up grain in the cities and guard it. The food will be a reserve supply for the country during the seven years of famine, which will strike Egypt. In this way the people will not starve."

The king and his officials approved this plan, and he said to them, "We will never find a better man than Joseph, a man who has God's spirit in him." The king then said to Joseph, "God has shown you all this, so it is obvious that you have greater wisdom and insight than anyone else. I will put you in charge of my country, and all my people will obey your orders. Your authority will be second only to mine. I now appoint you governor over all Egypt."

The king removed from his finger the ring engraved with the royal seal, and put it on Joseph's finger. He put a fine linen robe on him, and placed a gold chain around his neck. He gave him the second royal chariot to ride in, and his guard of honour went ahead of him and cried out, "Make way! Make way!" And so Joseph was appointed governor over all Egypt.

The king said to him, "I am the king—and no one in all Egypt shall so much as lift a hand or a foot without your permission."

He gave Joseph the Egyptian name Zaphenath Paneah, and he gave him a wife - Asenath, the daughter of Potiphera, a priest in the city of Heliopolis. Joseph was thirty years old, when he began to serve the king of Egypt. He left the king's court and travelled all over the land.

During the seven years of plenty, the land produced abundant crops, all of which Joseph collected and stored in the cities. In each city he stored the food from the fields around it. There was so much grain that Joseph stopped measuring it—it was like the sand of the sea."

That event was a divine inspired idea that put Joseph in the place of splendour and wealth creation.

Such showers of favours and opportunities in life are real, and they are channels of wellbeing, that must not be abused nor taken for granted. Yes, Joseph's childhood dreams of greatness came to pass, and his brothers and whole family came to bow and prostrate to his greatness and power in Egypt. Godly ideas are special golden chances of wealth creation.

IDEAS CREATION DIFFER IN LEVELS MASSIVELY FROM LACK OF EDUCATION TO FORMAL EDUCATION:

Creating ideas have levels, and differ in those with lack of education from others with formal education. They can both create resources, but the vocation and depth in creating wealth differs. A vocation can be defined as a person's main occupation or employment. It may also be a trade or profession.

When a person has a formal education in something, depending on the person's desires and ability, four things happen:

- the ability to think intelligibly in concepts becomes greater i.e. your sense of innovative ideas increases in greater dimension.

- you are able to assess the various gifts and talents embedded in you effectively: exposure to knowledge accelerates progress in this zone. You are able to do more than those who lack education.

- you are able to explore and learn quicker by investing in yourself: making extensive research in what you want to do, through studying and making enquiries to upgrade yourself in knowledge and understanding

- the person can become smart to spot opportunities and take advantage of certain circumstances.

- Like gold dust and mineral ores which have to go through processing through deep refining in water and fire to bring out the gold and pure minerals, formal education opens your intelligence better and leads you into modern technological systems.

Through formal education, we now have a world of the development of IT skills (Information Technology), diverse Computer softwares and other sophisticated modern technological industrial machine systems that have achieved economies of large scale productions in factory products and in various business practices, not to mention space exploration, the media world of "YouTube, Facebook, Instagram, Tiktok, as well as modern aircraft production that uses aerodynamics to fly in the clouds.

For example, a person with lack of education going into farming may do peasant farming, but with formal education and capital resources, it could take on a new turn into modern sophisticated techniques, combining modern technology and machine systems that take farming into greater heights, to the point of even processing the farm products into preserved packages on a large commercial scale with the same farm produce. This will certainly create greater and better and easier wealth generation than peasant farming. As the business becomes bigger and efficient, it gains economies of large scale production i.e. the cost of labour per output becomes less than that of a smaller enterprise or a beginner. It implies, for example, if it cost a small enterprise £100 to produce 20 bags of grain, the big Company with large resources and technological advancement can produce, say 30 bags using the same £100. That gives the bigger Company the competitive advantage to sell more and even reduce prices to dominate the market and capture a greater market share because their cost is comparatively cheaper.

PRACTICAL EDUCATED IDEAS, EXAMPLE 1: Dyson's British strawberries New Farming Technology in the UK.

According to the CEO, Sir James Dyson, "Dyson Farming is developing new approaches to efficient, high technology agriculture, which we hope will lead to a sustainable commercial future."

In their latest publication from their website, Dyson Farming has its new strawberries farm of 15-acre glasshouse in Carrington,

Lincolnshire. In doing so it supports the advancement of high-tech, sustainable farming in the UK, and avoids unnecessary food miles that come from imported strawberries at this time of the year.

The Glass Greenhouse farming is lengthening the British strawberry season by growing quality strawberries using advanced technological processes and machinery at a time of year, early spring and late autumn, when traditionally, British strawberries are in very short supply. This will contribute to the UK becoming more self-sufficient in food, reducing the air miles associated with imported fruit.

Powered with renewable electricity and surplus heat from Dyson Farming's adjacent anaerobic digester, the giant glasshouse is 424m long with 832 rows of strawberries and 700,000 strawberry plants which will produce 750 tonnes of strawberries each year for British consumers.

It is the latest addition to Dyson Farming's highly efficient circular farming approach, which has helped make the Dyson Farming business carbon neutral.

PRACTICAL EXAMPLE 2: Elon Musk's beginning business Idea.

One of the world's richest men, Elon Musk, I understand, studied physics and economics at the University of Pennsylvania, USA, but he later developed passion for Computer programming skills and taught himself to programme by reading books on "Basic programming language," which at that time, offered a six months course.

According to resource information in "Wikipedia.org", Elon Musk's entrepreneurial journey began in 1995, with the co-founding of Zip2, an online city guide with maps, directions, and yellow pages for newspapers. He and his brother Kimbal, with help from Greg Kouri, created the software and marketed it to printing publications companies like The New York Times and the Chicago Tribune. Below are further details:

In 1999, Zip2 was sold to Compaq Computer Corporation, for $307million, making Musk a multimillionaire, with his brother Kimbal picking his share. It was sold in cash and $34 million in stock options.

Their business Funding: Musk initially borrowed $28,000 from his father.

Business Location: It initially operated from a small rented office in Palo Alto, California.

Significance: This was Musk's first venture, demonstrating his ability to develop and market software, and build a successful business.

After selling Zip2, Musk then founded an online financial services company, X.com, which later became PayPal, which specialized in payments and transferring money online.

Today, besides other Investments, Elon Musk is the CEO and a significant Investor of the Electric Vehicle manufacturing Company called TESLA on a large commercial scale in USA. He is also the co-founder of PayPal, founder of Space X, and the person who acquired Twitter (now X) in 2022.

EXAMPLE 3. China's rise in Electronics

The country China now appears a market leader in electronics, but it all started with the early creating of ideas about the importance of electronics.

My research shows that China began a formal computing development program in 1956 when it launched the Twelve-

Year Science Plan, and formed the Beijing Institute of Computing Technology under the Chinese Academy of Sciences (CAS).

The industry rapidly evolved due to consistent determination and focus. Since 1980, China's electronics industry has experienced rapid growth, driven by economic reforms, open policies, and a strong demand for consumer electronics.

Today China sees a great boost as a market leader in smart phones, Laptop computers and diverse electronic gadgets and accessory products. This is the outcome of processing ideas through education.

EXAMPLE 4: Malaysia's Industrial breakthrough ideas under "Prime Minister Mahathir Mohamad."

According to resources from UC Davis Department of Economics, a research University in California, USA; Malaysia's industrial breakthrough was driven by a combination of factors, including establishing free trade zones, attracting foreign investment, and shifting from an agricultural economy to a manufacturing-based one. **The free trade zones which started in Penang and then around Kuala**

Lumpur, facilitated the transition from import-substitution industries to export-oriented manufacturing.

Under Prime Minister Mahathir Mohamad, the country experienced rapid economic growth and urbanization, with mega-projects like the Petronas Towers and the North-South Expressway being completed. Foreign investment, particularly from Japan, played a significant role in the development of heavy industries and the growth of exports.

All these are signs of expansion and development of ideas, with open imagination and intelligence for innovation.

EXAMPLE 5: New Testament Example: In ancient Israel, Jesus called and anointed some Apostles (Apostle means - the one who is sent on a mission).

Most of them were not formally educated but there was one, called Apostle Paul, who was called later to add to the original twelve. He happened to be a scholar, an intelligent man. Though the twelve did a good job, Paul was used a lot more, and he ended up writing the greater portion of the "New Testament books" in the Bible to the benefit of the world today. Thirteen (13) of the twenty seven(27) books of the New Testament are traditionally believed to be written by Paul the Apostle, which is more than the number ascribed to any other New Testament author. So education has greater advantages that bypass the uneducated.

NATURAL ENDOWMENT OF VISION AND PURPOSE:

Every human being has an inborn, innate natural passion to do or create something that generates resources and valuable assets.

There is always a link between a man's purpose, passion and desires in life. Psalms 37:4 says "delight yourself in the Lord, and He shall give you the desires of your heart."

These manifest themselves in our natural embedded abilities of gifts and talents. But you have to identify your desires and passions to create something or a service and to develop it. Desires create passion.

PASSION BRINGS ENERGY: Your passion is the drive that turns you on to pursue creativity, enabling you to knock at all possible doors and opportunities until you emerge successful.

WRITE DOWN YOUR IDEAS OF VISION, OR DREAMS: In other words, to keep track, it is always better to write down your vision and dreams, unless you are someone who has a long term memory to ingrain them in your mind. Yet there will come a time, when more details will be accumulated, and so having a journal to make notes will eventually be necessary otherwise many micro ideas and points could be lost and forgotten.

- **Get clear with your dreams and goals and write them down.** It gets you focused and memorable. It increases success that way.

Though, some may unconsciously not put it in writing, but may carry a mental picture of it all the time, many also drop it when circumstances outwit their plans.

However, fundamentally writing down your Vision gives you a frontlet of focus, a memory and thinking skills. In ancient Israel, the book of the Prophet Habbakuk said "The Lord gave me this answer saying, "Write down the vision on tablets, what I reveal to you, so that it can be read at a glance. Put it in writing, because it is not yet time for it to come true. But the time is coming quickly, and what I show you will come true. It may seem slow in coming, but wait for it; it will certainly take place, and it will not be delayed."

- **Your preparation in private vs. in public:** What you prepare or who you are in private is what takes you public.

In the past, before David killed Goliath, he was a shepherd boy, who was anointed by God through Samuel the Prophet. With this supernatural power, he managed to kill in private, Lions and Bears who came to attack any of the sheep in the fields. This caused him to develop skills and experience in private, to be able to take on the then giant Goliath in public. This public display of victory became a doorway, which gave David the opportunity to be loved and accepted to the Kingship position of Israel in those days.

OVERCOMING CHALLENGES: Challenges will come your way in your bid to pursue your dreams or vision. No one suddenly becomes successful in any pursuit. Your dreams and vision of success will go through various challenges and it takes a person of faith and determination to succeed. The determinants are:

1. **Be Laser focused,** let your vision consume your heart, mind and imagination. Having laser-focus increases your odds of success.

2. **Stepping Stones:** Until you get started, some little opportunities of jobs can be stepping stones. It does not mean stay idle in your room, waiting for the rains to come and not do anything else.

3. **Delay is not denial:** It may look like it will not succeed but it's all a matter of time, as you work on the dream, educate yourself in preparation and always be conscious of opportunities when they come. When they appear and you are not prepared, it's too late.

Just because things neither happened nor lined up the way and time you want them doesn't mean they won't happen. Keep your faith.

Secondly, Time: Things may not happen the time that you want them but don't panic. Because every dream has a gestation period i.e. it's like the process or period of developing inside the womb between conception and birth. In the fullness of time the baby will appear, the breakthrough will come. The book of Habbakuk 2:3 makes it clear saying, "For the vision is yet for an appointed time; at the end it will speak, and it will not lie. Though it tarries, wait for it; because it will surely come, it will tarry."

4. **Keep your dream to yourself** because not everyone will be interested to share your vision or ideas:

Know that not everyone is enthusiastic or interested in your dream like you. They may not have your similar gifts, talents and passion. So you would be better off keeping your dreams to yourself and pursue them.

Telling those who don't share your dream may limit your aspirations because they may tell you negative statements that will discourage you, if you are not determined about your goals.

Let determination, character and focus be in the arsenal of your mentorship. These are your array of innate resources.

5. **You will experience setbacks and several resistances.** No one gets all wrapped up from early stages, not even after, but you will learn from experiences, pick up skills, wisdom and understanding along the process and adapt to changes.

Adaptation is the seed of progress into success.

6. **A Godly Vision will always be seen to define your life.** So you need to be sensitive and smart enough to realise that and not quit. When the vision is kept clear, success will come with determination and diligence.

Some people come to the point of aborting their dreams because the forces of challenges and disappointments may be too much, but if you keep trusting in God, success will appear. In Psalm 46:10, we read God as saying "Be still, and know that I am God; I will be exalted among the nations, I will be exalted in the earth."

This text means that you can trust God during times of chaos: that He has the "Cards" of Authority to control all the circumstances, and that his plans will bring victory irrespective of what humans do.

NOTE: Speak your dream into being, calling things that be not, as if they are. That is how God created the World, by the Words of His mouth. Your voice is not only meant for communication but also for creativity. So speak positive words and have a positive belief system. This is what faith is, no negative words. It's the language of success. God by nature calls into existence things that do not exist, as if they already existed.

- Learn the habit of meditation, it broadens knowledge, and brings better understanding to make your agenda memorable and be able to initiate progress. The man Joshua was told by God not to allow the written Laws to depart from his mouth, but should meditate on them day and night, and observe carefully, to do according to all that is written in it. For then he can make his way prosperous, and will have good success.

- Study: Read books and articles about your plans or you may choose to do courses that relate to your dreams and purpose.

- Review your goals and dreams and adapt to the changing circumstances of the market to keep you on top of the game.

- Exercise yourself towards godliness, i.e. keep honesty, good behaviours and integrity. It gives you character. Physical exercise has some value, but godly exercise is valuable in every way, because it promises life both for the present and for the future. This is a true saying, to be completely accepted and believed.

- Keep a journal and write what you hear during your routines. It will be your reminders that keep you steady and help you maintain good progress.

- Don't let bad habits waste your time and stay put at where you do not have to settle as your last stop. That is, settling in your comfort zone of some convenient spot instead of pursuing on to achieve your will and heart's desire.

  - For example, **doing something you hate and yet settling with it:** Sometimes because of laziness and complacency, others develop the habit of settling in doing things they may not like to, although they know there is progress and better things ahead but they allow their flesh and the environment to limit them.

  - **Making TV your friend and avoiding anything productive:** You are rather denying yourself the opportunity to use your imagination to think and create ideas for success. You may experience the consequences of scarcity and want like an armed robber.

- **Avoid making excuses:** In ancient Hebrews times, the story is told of a man who threw a great banquette and invited many guests. However, when the banquet was ready, all the invited guests refuse to attend, making flimsy excuses about their worldly affairs, like 'I have bought a field and must go and look at it; please accept my apologies.' Another one also said, 'I have bought five pairs of oxen and am on my way to try them out; please accept my apologies.' Yet another further said, 'I have just gotten married, and for that reason I cannot come.' The host, frustrated by the rejections, ordered his servants to go out into the streets and alley ways to invite anyone they find, including the poor, lame, the cripple and the blind to fill the banquet hall.

The story is an illustration of God's plans of invitation to all people irrespective of race to His Kingdom which is like the banquet. The call and inclusion of the less esteemed in the society and the poor documents God's willingness to welcome anyone who responds to His call by faith and obedience. The call requires an active response and willingness to follow Jesus. Those who play the cards of excuses misses God's best in life.

- **A mind-set that dwells on the past** instead of looking at the life ahead of you and thinking of what your talents and skills can do, can shipwreck your dream. In the time past, we are told of how God's Angel had to rescue a man called Lot including the wife and the whole family from destruction in the City of the then "Sodom and Gomorrah". The instructions given them was not to turn their eyes back to the City but rather to forge ahead and go forward. However, out of curiosity of lust and disobedience, Lot's wife looked back along the way, and immediately became a pillar of salt.

The negative past will always blind you and give you an impaired vision. Don't dwell on your past errors and misfortunes. It can draw you back with hurt, bitterness and hinder you from thinking of innovative ideas and happiness.

EXPOSURE TO GREATNESS AND KNOWLEDGE IS A DOOR THAT INSTIGATES SUCCESS:

There may be people in the field of your passion who have made it to the top, or are in the process of making it happen. Learn from them, they can be your mentors. Read about them, listen to their success stories and let them encourage you.

Why? This exposes you to a new way of thinking and new approaches to broaden your vision and try something new to modernize your way of doing things.

There is wisdom in the saying that, "if someone becomes blessed and wealthy in your neighbourhood, it means there is wealth in your neighbourhood, and you can also tap into yours." It also means being wealthy and blessed is real, and it is not limited to one person but for all. Your ability to explore, positions you for it.

ACTION YOUR DREAMS: You cannot afford to sit down leisurely doing only very little and expect great things will magically appear. No. If you want something extraordinary, you have to do something you have never done. You have to be adventurous to action your dreams. Sitting down not doing anything to accomplish it, is just wishful thinking and a denial of success and investment opportunities.

Nobody just stumbles into success anyhow, without doing anything concrete or taking steps to achieve it.

The truth is, there's a big difference between wanting something and taking action to make it happen. Sometimes, fear, doubt, or procrastination sneak in and keep you stuck.

YOUR BIGGER DREAM VS YOUR SMALL ENVIRONMENT:

Don't be discouraged nor be deterred, if the environment you find yourself in, is smaller than your bigger dreams. In ancient Israel, Jesus was a carpenter in a small, obscure, poor, village of Nazareth. Even His own people did not believe in His dream of Supernatural divine powers, but He did not allow that to be a bother to Him. He kept His focus and courage and eventually actioned His dreams for success. He has become not only the Saviour of His people from eternal damnation but the whole world.

Investment has something to do with risk taking. For example, people who are unwilling to work to support themselves and their families are at risk of falling into poverty, lacking the necessities of life. Anyone who is unwilling to take risks will not become an investor.

There is a warning against the dangers of laziness and complacency: a little sleep, a little slumber, a little folding of the hands to rest, and poverty will come upon you like a robber, and "want" like an armed man. It describes someone who keeps putting off their responsibilities with the excuse of needing just a little more rest. Rather, remember that what you diligently schedule to do gets done. Dedication is a master key.

WORTY OF NOTE: When Ideas are not processed and pursued to manifest, they end up becoming just a wish floating in a world of day-dreaming.

THE SEED PRINCIPLE OF IDEAS :

Creation documents life as beginning with the idea of a Seed principle. Adam and Eve began as human seeds to produce more human beings.

Aside of that, they were also given physical seeds that produced food to run their lives. What can be sown is a seed.

A seed means the beginning. You reap a harvest by beginning to sow a seed. Unless you sow, you don't reap. That's the rule for Increase.

The idea originally given them in the beginning was, "See, I have given you every herb that yields seed which is on the face of all the earth, and every tree whose fruit yields seed; to you it shall be for food"

Life gains operates on the same principle.

You will recognize that the seed principle extends beyond literal seeds that the farmer sows.

In wisdom-wise, in real life, every action, every use of words and thoughts or investment and all efforts towards increase becomes seeds in themselves..

Every time you spend in doing something or any encouragement in yourself is a seed that will always produce greater returns or corresponding harvest, positive or negatively.

So an "idea" is a seed you conceive and nurture. But you should handle it with great care in practical terms, because it has a future embedded in it. It can be a wealth of knowledge and understanding heading towards fruition.

RAISING FINANCE FOR YOUR DREAM PROJECT: the capital needed to start your Vision varies and it depends on the nature of the investment.

Some service industries are less capital intensive than others. Industrial projects follow the same sequence. In both cases, every project, from initial stages, often begins small, and in most cases as an individual venture, and increases as it gains acceptance in the market and becomes efficient and effective.

Raising capital comes in various shapes and ways and they include:

1. Building savings of money from jobs that you may be doing, and using it to invest on pilot scheme basis to increase capital. You may take up some jobs as stepping stones to achieve your dream goal

2. Fund raising as you sell your vision to potential Philanthropists and Charities or family sources.

3. Financial institutions like banks and building societies can sponsor the vision depending on the viability of the project. Of course, they will demand what is called "business plan and cash flow projection over a period of time, say the next five years."

4. When it comes to book writing and publishing for example, it depends more on the ideas you have, your thoughtfulness and skills in developing manuscripts. With some savings and a little bank support if needed, you can get it published and put it on the market.

IT'S NOT HOW MUCH OF WHAT YOU HAVE BUT HOW YOU DEVELOP IT: Increase in life comes like a mustard seed growing. A mustard seed is the smallest of all the seeds, but when it's sown on the ground, it grows to become one of the largest trees, and birds of the air come and make their nests and home in it. The tree's expansion attracts other advantages that impact life. Your wealth creation will eventually attract others who want to join you to work for you.

The principle of the farmer is a concept of sowing and reaping which our God given nature develops internally when the farmer does his bit of ploughing, tilling the ground and sowing the right seeds.

The idea goes like this, the farmer sows seeds in a field, the seeds are tiny and small in nature; these are choice quality seeds of various crops. The farmer sleeps at night and is up and around during the day. Yet the seeds keep sprouting and growing, and he does not even understand how. It is the ground which is now the seed developer. It's the ground that makes the decision to let the seeds sprout and grow into plants that produce grain. Then, when harvest season comes and the grain is ripe, the farmer puts in the knife for the harvest. In these modern days of industrial technology, combine harvesters are used in large scale farming, giving them economies of large scale production.

So, it's all about the ability to develop your thinking. Ideas call for development. Undeveloped ideas go under the carpet and nothing happens. Wealth opportunity is here wasted away. The more you pass over opportunities regularly, the more wealth slips away, and the more want hits at your door.

When minerals of gold, silver, rubies or copper are first mined or dug from the ground, initially you might think it's just a rocky soil but it's got potential wealth in them. It has to undergo processing until the pure mineral appears.

Ideas are always conceived and nurtured or nursed on pilot scheme basis, testing their innovation process, any shortcomings and adjustments, until finally, perfection is achieved.

You may not get it off successfully all at one go. Every project is not going to be a blanket success immediately. Like a baby learning to walk, there can be humps and bumps along the way. You will make mistakes, disappointments may come, some areas can fail, but they are not necessarily long lasting.

In all cases you will learn from experiences, skills will be acquired and lessons will be learnt. Like an engineer, you learn new and better ways of handling things.

When babies eventually learn to walk with strength and agility, they never fall back anymore. Any successful business person will have gone through a period of setbacks of some sort. So never give up when facing ups and downs in your endeavours.

For example, many banks may reject your application for support, but as you keep putting your accounts in order and keep on persisting, you will eventually get someone who will open up to you.

When wealth is passed on to someone as inheritance, I will not classify it as success. The ability to manage, maintain and grow the wealth will determine the person's skills, sustainability and prosperity.

GOAL SETTING

Goals are the future targets you aim to hit in order to achieve your dreams or desires. For example, your desire may be to become the head of a company or to be a successful investor or entrepreneur.

Goals are what you want to do within a specific range of time to achieve that dream or vision. Technically, goals are dreams with deadlines attached.

"With everything there is time involved. There is time to plant and time to reap. There is also time to invest and time to make gains. The human life deals with time. You cannot avoid it."

In the ancient days, the man named Noah was given goal setting in pictures, a Vision regarding the building of a Wooden Ark which was to be constructed and would be their safety home against an impending flood which was going to destroy all possessions on the earth including all humans because of sin.

He was not told the date and time of the flood to come, but he documented the dream in his heart and mind, and pursued it to complete the Ark building. It was some time after the vision of the Wooden Ark had been built, that God asked him to get on board with all his family and his possessions. For forty days and forty nights, the flood ravaged the earth to total destruction, whilst the Ark sailed safely on the flooded waters until eventually, the storms subsided and the Ark finally landed at a safe place on a mountain top.

When you pursue a goal clearly with all the diligence, things get done and success will appear. Whatever you focus on gets done.

SET UP SMART EFFICIENT GOALS: The word "SMART" can be explained better, when it is turned into an acronym "S.M.A.R.T."

That means your goals must be "S" specific to bring clarity into it, e.g. you must be clear if you want to save say, £10,000 or £15,000 a year.

"M" means it must be measurable, that is, it can truly be assessed and a value put on it when the goal is reached or achieved.

"A" is attainable, act on your dreams if there is a probability, that you can attain it.

"R" is, it must be realistic, talking about what you can truly set as possible you can do, not something outside your realm of possibility. That is, for example, do not claim you can save huge money at the bank when you have not been able to control your spendthrift nature.

Finally, "T" is setting a time line. It motivates you as a driving force. Set your deadlines and pray over your goals.

PUT YOUR GOALS INTO WRITING AND AIM AT FOCUS:

- Action initiates the beginning of success.
- Do not set too many goals at a time, as your strengths can be depleted or fritter away because you are not superhuman: then activities can be wearying and confusing with your limited resources.
- Starting with about five goals every time can be reasonable and memorable.

Set a few at a time so you can focus enough strength on them otherwise, your attention will be scattered all over the place.

Set goals that are memorable: Clear written goals. Clarity makes it easier, memorable that is. Clarity gives you a better future. Ask questions about your future, e.g., where you want to be, for example, what you want to do in two to three years' time. You can only go as far as you can see or imagine.

- **Be specific and trust God, however big the dream is, and keep it at your frontlet:** What you think about, you move towards it.

- **Build good habits that create progress on a consistent basis:** How do you start, what capital and resources will you need, what level of knowledge and education of the project will you need? Who are those to connect with?

- **Motivate yourself by having a preview of your future success, imagine it:** If you don't know where you are going, you never get to your future, your Canaan's land. You may rather end up going around in circles and never achieve anything substantial. The person may end up just looking for something to get by.

For example, over 2000 years ago, before His arrest, Jesus celebrated a preview of His victory on the "Cross of Crucifixion" when as He entered Jerusalem, the crucifixion city, He intentionally paraded Himself riding on a donkey as a Victory sign and the multitude of celebrants laid their clothes and palm branches on the floor, as the red carpet, before Him and shouting praises of Kingship, "Praise the Son of David, Blessed is He who comes in the name of the Lord." Jesus knew that He will be arrested and crucified as if the victory is destroyed, but on the third, as He responded in a resurrection from the grave, the victory was regained. Yes, in your life ventures, you must be confident of success in sight. That keeps you always bubbling with energy and joy. That should be your preview exercise.

Keep a journal for your goals: Most high achievers have the habit of keeping a journal for their goals. Write down various developments and progress report. Such record keeping puts you on track to trace the **monitoring of the progress of your goals and review them on consistent**

basis: see how and what work is going on, and how much progress is being made, and make adjustments when it comes. Avoid negligence of important issues that need urgent attention and changes. Adaptation is the seed for progress.

Short term and Long term goal:

There are two sets of goals both of which help together to achieve your dreams and aspirations.

These are what is called, "Short term goals and Long term goals"

Short terms goals: are things that you want to do and achieve within a short time, and which you lay as a foundation or act as the helper to achieve your bigger vision. It could begin on a pilot scheme basis and monitor progress.

Timewise, normally they are things you negotiate in yourself to achieve in months or within a year. Technically, they become like stepping stones to your future. For example, you may want to do some odd jobs or other jobs as you wait for the opportunity to launch yourself into what you consider as your future. It can also be doing some voluntary jobs to gain some skills and experiences.

Most times, people do such things unconsciously in their hearts and minds, but if you are knowledgeable about this wisdom key, it keeps you on the alert, comported and settles your heart from worry and anxiety. It's a process in life that sometimes you have to undertake.

Long term goals: require careful planning and strategies because they are your ultimate long run aspiration that you cannot achieve within a few months. In sporting terms, it's a marathon not a sprint. It takes enough time and preparation to get on board. It links you with something you see as more permanent a dream to reach.

These are plans that take enough preparation, training and especially education. For example, you may want to earn a University degree.

Most long term goals require favour. Sometimes you may need to wait for opportunities of favour to come. If that is so, you must package yourself with excellence, good behaviours and attitude. Favour opens unexpected doors of riches.

It may even need ample time to make sure you acquire some bank savings to boost your credit score for financial aid from the bank.

If education is involved, it will demand more time and space. You are talking about maybe a year, five years or even more.

FINDING A MARKET: ASKING THROUGH ADVERTISING

Nobody will know what you have or want to sell until you make it known. Reach out to your buyers. That is it. Even if you have properties to rent, the potential client, is a buyer. It is about finding a way to make known what you produce for people who will need and want them. It comes by exploring the market and making your presence known.

In other words, find a way to tell others about what you have to sell, and say how good and beneficial it is for their lives, and finally ask them to buy, using all encouraging available means.

In other words, find a way to advertise your product or service industry to others. In advertising, you are asking your way out to success. Asking is a success principle.

For example, no charity organization can raise funds without asking. In much the same way, a business organization cannot go big without finding a way to make their products or services known to potential customers and clients. You have to advertise yourself. Even most small businesses and enterprises advertise themselves indirectly with the good quality work they do, their reputation. Their clients advertise them to their friends, families and neighbours by word of mouth.

And so asking is a success principle. Keeping quiet, confined and keeping your service or product to a corner and not making your presence widely known, is not expansion.

There is wisdom about knowledge expressed in the scriptures which says, "Ask, and you will receive; seek, and you will find; knock, and the door will be opened to you. For everyone who asks will receive, and anyone who seeks will find, and the door will be opened to those who knock." Then again it goes further to say that if you do not ask, you will not receive.

In ancient Egypt, when God was calling Moses, He advertised it in a burning bush. In so doing, He was asking him to come and see, and at the same time to hear something which he will eventually take along to "sell the message of deliverance" to his people in Egypt.

Moses saw a burning bush, but the tree and leaves were not consumed. Being curious, he decided to approach it to see such a strange site. Suddenly, he heard a voice in the bush fire that gave him direction and a profession with divine Authority to go to Egypt, and lead his people out to the promised land flowing with milk and honey. The advert changed his life and destiny. God achieved His plans of success. That was an advertising technique.

Some other advertising techniques: This means employing the appropriate advertising ways that ensure viewers will be attracted to your brand and remember it.

- **Attention Catchers:** An advert is something that should attract your attention to a product or a service. It may not even be related to the product or service being sold. In the above incident with the burning bush experience, the said advert was not related to the assignment he was given nor the purpose for which he was called. The site of a strange burning bush with the bush not being consumed by the fire was to attract Moses's attention to listen to the message about the mission.

- **Colour:** people are attracted by colour in adverts, especially the women and children. There is a vast difference in attention between an advert which is set in dull unattractive colours than with brighter colours. The above incident of the burning bush with Moses, can be seen to be spotted quickly because fire flames have a glittering colour output as well as make a tinkling fire sound to attract your attention.

- **Design & packaging:** In advertising and marketing terms, the way you design your product and quality of packaging tells the story of either attraction or rejection. What the eye beholds as nice becomes a magnet to the potential customer.

- **Celebrity endorsements:** In this form of adverts, well known celebrities are constantly announced and pictured with a product or service as having endorsed it as good or using it. Psychologically, it identifies the product as good for purchase. Psychologically, it is saying that if a famous person is buying it, it's also good for you to make a purchase. And it works all the more especially if the product is good in quality.

- **Promotions and Special offers:** Sales promotions are marketing activities which are created temporarily to boost awareness, motivate sales and to increase customer loyalty. They involve activities like price discounts, vouchers, coupons, free samples and "prize draws" by creating winning numbers in a raffle-style form for customers who make specific targeted items. Winners are rewarded with prizes like special merchandise or a gift card and many other rewards available.

- **Use of Pricing Psychology:** this is about pricing your produce a few pence lower than other sellers eg £99.50 price instead of £100. It takes the potential customer's mind-set from £100 to the £90 price range. Though the margin is small, psychologically it has the potential of swaying the mind of the customer especially if the price in other shops is reading £100 when the quality looks the same.

- **Sponsoring a TV programme:** In sponsorship programmes, the product brand is mentioned either on the TV or on the Radio as the one sponsoring that programme. The intention is to create awareness and link potential customers to the product.

For example, on a United Kingdom ITV1 programme called Britain's Got Talent, a Tesco Supermarket will show their products alongside their discount "Club Card" and will announce their "Club Card" as sponsoring the programme "Britain's Got Talent." On such a popular TV programme, it attracts greater audience.

In the same vein in the year 2025, during weather time broadcast on the "Sky News," Qatar Airways aeroplane flashes on the TV screen as the airline that "sponsors the weather." They are advertising the airline as popular and reliable to travel with.

Market Review and feedbacks: These are most times necessary because it tells what both buyers and customers feel and think about the product or services being offered to them. It helps the investor to adapt from the feedback and tie their products to the needs and requirements of customers.

Remember that in business terms, the customer is branded as "always right" because they bring in the money. So customers need to be respected. Hence it's worthy to develop customer care training for your staff and all workers under the umbrella of your business or Investment enterprise.

MANAGING SUCCESSFUL IDEAS OF WEALTH

Business is built to last, built for years and not seasons. Wealth does not stay permanent without proper care, and so good management skills are important. You must excel to manage it. Effective management is a door to longevity. And it takes determination and fortitude to excel.

You cannot take things for granted and stay average in your doings. You must put excellence in your heart at the behest of your business undertakings instead of being average. If you will not think average and behave average, the results will not be average but excellent.

Managing wealth is to map out or identify some key elements that bring success to your business ideas. These include:

- **Innovation:** Business innovation is all about developing new distinguishing ideas, services, processes, and products to inspire growth in the business network. Not only does it add value but it improves efficiency in the organization. This helps to increase revenue and reduce cost when efficiency is achieved. The ultimate idea behind innovation is to satisfy customer expectation and increase the catchment area of the market, technically to increase market share.

Innovation does not only mean developing only your new ideas, but most times to adopt new technologies created by other engineers in the industry. New technologies helps you stay ahead of the curve in the industry and gain advantages in market share.

Staying ahead of the curve is normally used in business technology and in the areas of innovation. It speaks of advancement in modern terms and having a proactive approach to leadership in the market. Being diligent to ensure excellence and consistency is a masterpiece in wealth creation.

In Ancient Israel time, God laid emphasis on efficiency, diligence and excellence to Joshua, the leader of His people as they headed to the Promised Land, saying, "this

Book of the Law shall not depart from your mouth, but you shall meditate in it day and night, observing to do according to all that is written in it. For then you will be prosperous, and enjoy good success."

- **Customer Satisfaction:** In managing wealth, we must attach importance to customer care and feed backs to know what satisfies them. The ability to identify the shortcomings of your produce or services you provide gives you the need to improve upon it and thus able to maintain customer loyalty. Such feedback is obtained through customer surveys by asking. Asking is a success principle.

Satisfying customer expectation is also to modernise your steps, your style, your brand and services to enable you become competitive in the market.

It calls for more research for information of knowledge and understanding of what you want to produce or are producing. Read the market and test your product or services from various angles and examine their strengths and weakness e.g., car manufacturers have to test how robust the vehicle is on rough roads and observe the suspensions and shock absorbers, as well as various parts that will be affected by many years of shaking and pressures of weight and adverse forces.

Aeroplanes have to be tested in the air to check the effect of aerodynamics i.e. how it can navigate through the movement of wind and storms. It's a key part of aviation science, affecting the design, performance, and safety of aircraft.

Also in ancient Israel, biblical records indicate that King David, a King of success, shepherded his people with integrity of heart. He led his people with skilful hands (Psalm 78:72).

- **Aim at Efficiency, avoid Waste and Control theft:** This is all about using resources effectively to achieve your goals. The aim is to develop the ability to maximise out, by targeting to reach the highest possible results with the available resources you possess.

Maximising out implies finding an efficient process in working and coordinating the business for profit. For example:

- In trading it's about stocking quality brand products and ensuring product availability on time.
- In factories and in any industry, it's about running efficient machine systems that give great output per the hour and per day.
- In the office places, it's about having the right efficient working system that produces results and managing staff work flow effectively.
- Where purpose is not known, abuse is inevitable. And so developing effective staff training methods at work places is an asset.
- Structure workflows and procedures to prevent redundancies and enhance productivity.
- For better productivity, equip employees with skills and develop efficient processes to produce results.
- Make effective use of resources in terms of raw materials, capital and labour to generate revenue.
- You must be able to check and measure efficiency and to assess

progress i.e. ensuring productivity and returns on capital or investments as well as energy usage should be calculated in principle.

- It's also about ensuring security against theft and disorder. Order is the proper arrangement of things. Wealth must be protected because the enemy lurks around like a roaring lion looking for loopholes to plunder and destroy. For example cyber-attacks are frequent these days around the world. In localised areas in our communities, business enterprises can go bankrupt because of corruption and stealing. Businesses must guard against theft.

- **Aim at Growing your business to catch a broader audience:** The saying goes that little drops of water create a mighty ocean. The broader the customer base, the wealthier the establishment will be. When profits however little, are multiplied, they grow great wealth.

Thus enlarging your market increases your wealth: Even the scriptures confirm this principle, "Make the tent you live in larger; lengthen its ropes and strengthen the pegs! You will extend your boundaries on all sides; your people will get back the land that the other nations now occupy. Cities now deserted will be filled with people." (Isaiah 54:2-3 GNT). So dream wide because God is bigger than your imagination and dreams.

- **Be Adaptable to changes:** to be adaptable is a game changer in the market as it brings advantages to your business. Other competing products and services are entering the market all the time with new ideas of customer taste and packaging. So you must be smart to adapt to changes in market conditions and people's concerns.

- **Observe Time Management:**
  - Develop a Consistent Planner
  - Schedule your task
  - When overwhelmed, it implies set realistic goals
  - When faced with too many distractions, it is telling you to be attention focused.
  - Do not do things anyhow or at the wrong moments or time

- Make faith filled declarations, it's called the language of success, stay positive all the time.

- **Emphasis on Team Work:** You must always encourage people working for you to work as a team. Team work is employees working together to complete a task or achieve a goal. This is beneficial because it taps into the various skills and viewpoints of individuals to increase productivity and efficiency. Two are better than one because they have a good return for their labour.

The key elements that ensure effective team work are:

- One vision and same goals in getting a better output.

- To build trust in each other and enable common sharing of ideas and listening.

- Open communication, not only to share information but also to solve conflicts. This is very important because impatience and infighting are barriers to success.

- Mobilise collective skills to advantage.

- Team work mobilises faith of each other: there is strength and confidence in unity, and all these give drive to efficiency and productivity.

In ancient days in the land of Canaan we see Team work as Abraham and his Servant cooperate with God in close partnership to find a wife for Isaac, Abraham's son. His servant got to a village where he had to make a choice for a woman, who had to marry Isaac. He had to team up in prayer with God and he succeeded in getting the right choice. Team work embraces different abilities and strengths to get things done in a strong and efficient way.

- **Staff Training:** staff training is pivotal to the running of any business. You either train or the business will fall.

Staff training basically is a framework or a structure of education at the work place where employees are given knowledge, skills and guidelines of how the work place system operates. It's about harnessing the potentials of your employees through effective guidelines.

This is very important because where purpose is not known, abuse is the result.

Even when a graduate is first employed at the work place, the person has to be taken through a series of induction about the job and how the place operates and who to liaise with effectively.

In doing so, it promotes business productivity and also reduces cost by avoiding waste and abuse of resources.

Training creates awareness of the needs and resources of the organization, so that employees can adapt to changes especially to new technologies.

Employees must be taught customer care because in business, "the customer is termed to be always right." Why? Because they bring in the money, however small it is. Little drops of water create a mighty ocean.

The training helps employees to be tolerant towards impatient customers and know how to deal with the arrogant type. So listening attentively and good communication skills should be part of the training process.

Employees are sometimes trained on the job by working alongside existing colleagues. There are also off-the-job training courses or workshops where knowledge is imparted outside work environment.

WHEN IDEAS OF WEALTH ARE BLESSED:

When a person is blessed, it takes their creative abilities, ideas and wealth development into a greater and consistent dimension. Everything falls into place; they get better even when others are struggling. It's like in the ancient days when the people of Israel had to move from Egypt into the land of blessing, which was Canaan's land. Scriptural records indicate that their clothes and sandals did not wear out even after circling in the wilderness for forty years.

To be blessed means essentially empowerment to do well, to excel and be protected. It comes as a package of good fortune, favours and a shield of protection.

The source of blessings is most times divine or has Spiritual implications. The humans can also pronounce their blessing upon you, as a sign of approval upon your dealings or decisions. These are lines of favours and opportunities.

Divine favour comes as a manifestation of God's grace, leading to opportunities beyond one's own ability. Sometimes you need both the favour of God and that of "man"(the human), because the person may be the one holding the key of approval.

WORTHY OF NOTE: Favour comes as a "Title Given" and paves the way of protocol that you walk through. You do not struggle in it. It speaks for you.

- Godly favour is wonderful because in a mysterious way, it can bring you increases when others are decreasing.

- You can have the world's best without paying the price. So learn how to seek God's favour and appropriate it. It can be there for the rest of your life.

- It opens doors that man cannot close, however much the enemy tries to resist. The door is Spiritually protected to shame the jealous and the hater.

- Godly favour can be the solution or answer to all the chaos of this world. So it's a great virtue and a door of power.

- It gives you mandate over your circumstances even in times of adversity and challenges. In ancient times of Canaan's land, one Isaac faced famine and economic recession. But he listened to divine instructions and depended on God's favour to overcome the adversity and headed towards becoming rich and became very rich. Favour can overturn every bad economy.

- The blessing and favour come when God comes in. He says, "I will be with you." In the olden days in Egypt, it took one Joseph placed in a pit by his brothers, because of hatred of greatness in him, sold into slavery by them, thrown into prison in Egypt, and from prisoner to the position of a Governor, because he was the only person who was able to interpret the King's dream. According to the dream, disaster was coming and it was Joseph who had the keys to the solutions.

- Favour can take you from the least recognised to an unexpected management position.

- It can bring promotion in a person's life even though they don't have the expertise or seniority. Especially when people say to you, "I don't know why I'm doing this for you, but I wish to give this position to you or sell this to you at a discounted price."

- You may argue that's preferential treatment? Well, that's what favour brings. The rules of throne ascendancy were changed from being a Prince to give Joseph, a foreigner, the chance for Governorship.

- Blessings of favour fought the battle for him. He didn't think of fighting for anything. He just walked through the corridors of power.

- Favours are doors of opportunities to showcase your gifts and talents and we must be careful not to abuse it when the chance is given. It is an opportunity to excel and maintain integrity. There is a scriptural saying that, "When you sit down to eat with someone important, keep in mind who he is. If you have a big appetite for delicacies, restrain yourself. Don't be greedy for the fine food he serves; he may be trying to trick you."(Proverbs 23:1-3 GNT)

WORTHY OF NOTE: Blessings speed up the process of progression to a bountiful harvest which cannot be explained. Such blessings come through Godly Obedience and righteous living.

- It opens and exposes you to advantages in the market: It brings in people that you don't even know, to be of help to you.

- Seeing doors of favour open relaxes the nerves, because it takes the hassle and stress away.

KEEP GOOD CONDUCT: INTEGRITY

Business conduct in practical life is like being a good steward in charge of services and responsibilities in a King's Palace. It is required of stewards that they become faithful and serve with integrity to keep their place or position.

Business Integrity is about building a culture of being honest in what you stand for, whether in public or in private, committing to doing what you say you will do. It's about staying true to your standards of performance and being transparent about your shortcomings, being accountable and admitting your faults.

Know what you stand for in your dealings with your customers, suppliers, employees and business partners or shareholders.

Shoddy thinking: A business may initially start producing the right, good quality products and services, but after a while they lose sight of quality and go shoddy, thinking that the market will still love them and buy into their lack of integrity and concern. Not long after, the market is lost. Staying faithful is a magnet for success.

Character: You can rise high but what keeps you there is integrity, integrity in character, attitude and skills, as well as integrity in quality services. **Dishonest gain brings down a business or a good position.**

WORTHY OF NOTE: A person gets established in righteous living and upholding justice. A good name is more desirable than great riches, and to be esteemed is better than silver or gold. So we must learn to close any gaps between our intentions and actions.

SOME SCALE OF PRACTICES OF INTEGRITY IN BUSINESS: First and foremost, it's a decision making to create a standard of ethical principles of conduct and develop a brand image around the business. That's why business brand names like Gucci, Louis Vuitton, Apple, Google, Coca Cola, iPhone, Microsoft, Range Rover, Nike, can maintain their fame or popularity.

The principle is to put in place some ethical conducts that will create a good standard of operation for the business in relationship with customers, employees and investors. If you are a sole-proprietor, it means you have to be true to yourself. Who you are in private is what will show in public. Some of these business practices are:

- **Transparency:** being truthful and honest. Avoid malpractices and gain-sayings. Adopt open communication i.e., willingness to hear employees and customer complaints and unhappiness.

- **Be Adaptable to change:** adaptation is a seed for progress, otherwise you will fall behind and lose your market share. It comes through listening to feedbacks which you do through market survey and making changes, to enable you be ahead of the curve.

- **Maintain Trust:** keep it at your frontlet. If others can trust you, they want to share secret affairs with you that can cover up potential shortfalls or put you ahead in business.

- **Honour Customers and Clienteles:** these include buyers, employees and suppliers alike. When respect or honour are put in place, they create peace and satisfaction. It creates customer loyalty.

- **Obedience to regulatory laws** governing businesses and industrial set-ups e.g., Government and community operation rules and laws. It keeps you in peace and prevents lawsuits and cost to the detriment of the enterprise.

- **Keeping promises and responsibilities:** these are simply the out stretch of integrity. Put into practice what you promise and fulfill it. It advertises honesty and creates employee commitment and customer satisfaction.

- **Keeping to ethical conduct:** keep good moral behaviours in the business whilst you monitor corruption, stealing, bribery, rude behaviours towards customers and among colleagues. If good values and standards become a framework in the business, it enables employees and all staff comport themselves to create an atmosphere for progress.

- **Create a norm of accountability** by accepting your mistakes, address issues that may arise and design creative ways to resolve them. People sympathise with that cultural attitude and can cooperate with any shortfalls.

Although blessed, mismanagement can ruin a laudable business venture. So it ties in with the saying that when purpose is not known, abuse is inevitable. Blessings come as a package of wisdom and knowledge, so you cannot bypass these virtues. Be opened to seek wisdom and let knowledge be pleasant to your soul. Wisdom is simply divine intelligence. Don't underestimate them in wealth development.

"When wisdom enters your heart, and knowledge is pleasant to your soul, discretion will preserve you, and understanding will keep you".

DEVELOP A GIVING HABIT:

Giving is an intrinsic part of our created human nature, we were born with it. You will realize that when you practise it as a habit and become cultured into it, it carries a blessing. The word "blessed" is in a nutshell empowerment to prosper.

You will realize that from the beginning of creation, man was imbued or impregnated with **the idea and principle of Giving:** And God said to Adam and Eve, "See, I have **Given** you every herb that yields seed which is on the face of all the earth, and every tree whose fruit yields seed; to you it shall be for food. Also, to every beast of the earth, to every bird of the air, and to everything that creeps on the earth, in which there is life, I have **Given** every green herb for food." (Genesis 1:29-30 NKJV)

The pronouncement of the Giving act, gave man the chance to grow, multiply and increase in resources. The human world population today has increased to over eight billion. The current world wealth of knowledge, technological advancement and resources of financial wealth cannot all be measured. Money is being counted in over trillions and trillions of dollars, pounds, sterling, euros, Chinese Yuan, Russian Rouble, Japanese Yen and in all other nations' currencies.

Today almost every nation in the world sees the need for giving to support others in need. In the yearly budget of many nations, funds are allocated as "foreign aid" to help the under privileged because they want them to also thrive and get a better life. Scholarships are being given as aid to students to study and do innovative things in order to upgrade their lives.

Various Charity organizations have opened all over the world to, "Give funds and material support to areas that need them," with the aim of helping the needy. Today, there is the United Nations Aid, individual companies' charity funds, and private individual's aid e.g., Bill Gates, a billionaire, is a renowned philanthropist.

Giving incentives to your employees in the form of yearly bonus, however little, is a seed for motivation. Not only does it inspire them to perform better but they also surround you with love.

If someone loves you, they tell you hidden secrets about what they see regarding the business and any malpractices going on in the dark to undermine your business. All these work together to drive growth.

One of the memorable giving stories in history is about a man called Abraham: Scriptural records indicate that God called him out of his country to give him a promised land called Canaan. His obedience awarded him riches of Silver, Gold and multitudes of livestock on that land. But his wife, Sarah, was barren and could not give birth. Whilst in prayer God promised to give him a child who was to be called Isaac. As the child grew, God tested Abraham's obedience to Him.

Then God said, "Take now your son, your only son Isaac, whom you love, and go to the land of Moriah, and offer him there as a burnt offering on one of the mountains of which I shall tell you."(Genesis 22:2)

To my surprise, Abraham was not at all hesitant, but obeyed without any preconditions. But at the place of the sacrifice, the moment he stretched out his hand and took the knife to slay his son, he heard the voice of an Angel to stop.

And this is the most exciting part, the Angel said "By Myself I have sworn, says the Lord, because you have done this thing, and have not withheld your son, your only son from me, I will bless you, and I will multiply your descendants as the stars of the heaven and as the sand which is on the seashore; and your descendants shall possess the gate of their enemies. In your seed all the nations of the earth shall be blessed, because you have obeyed My voice."

This was a massive, awesome incident of giving by faith, the effects of which still inspire people in the world today, to give out of love as a principle for increase.

WORTHY OF NOTE: The generous will themselves be blessed, for they share their food with the poor (Proverbs 22:9). In managing wealth, we can learn to be like God, being kind hearted. Giving cheerfully to the needy and to the less able will bring blessings to the business.

WE CAN ALL HAVE A FRESH START:

I perceive we can all adjust to a new rejuvenated mindset for a fresh start because creation permits us to do so. To someone reading this today, it may be time to have reflections of the past, readdress your thinking habits and update some ideas and vision.

Potential good dreams that might have been abandoned or allowed to linger on procrastination can now be revived.

ANOTHER BOOK FROM THE AUTHOR

Developing Warmth In Relationships

- A good relationship should always be warming up to keep the warmth that has been achieved-

These two books by the Author are life changing materials

AUTHOR'S BIO

Rev. Ernest Sarfo is the Senior Minister-in-Charge of Life Interchange Ministries, a registered Christian Charity in the United Kingdom.

He is also a product of the University of East London and Spurgeon's Bible College, both in the United Kingdom.

ACKNOWLEDGEMENTS

I here want to show my appreciation to my wife, Irene Sarfo, and my daughter, Abigail Sarfo, whose supportive ministries and encouragement have contributed greatly to this development.

LICC TEAM SUPPORT: Also to be remembered are all the four Ministers and the entire members of Life Interchange Christian Centre (LICC), whose love continues to sustain a warm relationship that made this happen.

PROOFREADING: I want to honour in Proofreading, the services of Mr Anthony Gambrah, the CEO of "Valuation & Estate Services" and the former Lecturer of KNUST (University of Science & Technology, Ghana)